The Agile Manager's Guide To

INFLUENCING PEOPLE

By John R. Hook

Velocity Business Publishing
Bristol, Vermont USA

For Pat—True Hero

Copyright © 1999 by John R. Hook
All Rights Reserved
Printed in the United States of America
Library of Congress Catalog Card Number 99-64996
ISBN 1-58099-015-0
Title page illustration by Elayne Sears

If you'd like additional copies of this book or a catalog of books in the Agile Manager Series™, please get in touch.

■ **Write us:**
Velocity Business Publishing, Inc.
15 Main Street
Bristol, VT 05443   USA

■ **Call us:**
1-888-805-8600 in North America (toll-free)
1-802-453-6669 from all other countries

■ **Fax us:**
1-802-453-2164

■ **E-mail us:**
info@agilemanager.com

■ **Visit our Web site:**
www.agilemanager.com

The Web site contains much of interest to business people—tips and techniques, business news, links to valuable sites, and electronic versions of titles in the Agile Manager Series.

Contents

Books in the Agile Manager Series™:

Giving Great Presentations
Understanding Financial Statements
Motivating People
Making Effective Decisions
Leadership
Goal-Setting and Achievement
Delegating Work
Cutting Costs
Influencing People
Effective Performance Appraisals
Writing to Get Action
Hiring Excellence
Building and Leading Teams
Getting Organized
Extraordinary Customer Service
Customer-Focused Selling
Managing Irritating People
Coaching to Maximize Performance

Introduction

Wouldn't you like to be more effective in dealing one-on-one with others, more persuasive in moving them to your point of view? This book will help you achieve that increased effectiveness. It will give you precisely the set of tools and techniques you need to get your way in sensitive matters in both your professional and personal lives. Consider these typical situations:

- Convincing your boss to let you try something promising, but risky.
- Persuading a good subordinate to accept a transfer, a downgrade, or maybe even a challenging upgrade.
- Pushing a subordinate to a higher level of performance.
- Requesting something for yourself: a raise, choice assignment, special training, or transfer to a new city.
- Convincing your family of the wisdom of requesting or accepting a transfer.

The list of such situations is endless. You've been there, you know—and they all call for a high degree of persuasive ability.

The skills you need fall into four categories:

Negotiation: The overall process of designing a strategy to get what you want and setting the tone for discussions. It also includes careful consideration of whether or not to attempt to persuade.

Influence: A soft approach in which you try to educate others to your point of view through logic, an appeal to their emotions or values, or through joint development of a solution or course of action.

Power: A tougher approach—you use it when influence fails, yet when getting your way is essential.

Conflict Management: Dealing with differences in viewpoint throughout the negotiation process.

This book will provide you specific tools and techniques in each of these areas. The ideas are presented concisely and clearly, and they are reinforced by examples you'll relate to your own experience. With these approaches in hand, you will feel confident planning an encounter with even the most difficult adversary, and I'll bet you come out a winner more often than not.

Note: The approach here has been thoroughly tested with practicing managers. I was first introduced to the notion of deliberately planning influence efforts by Dr. Frank Sherwood, founding director of the Federal Executive Institute (a training facility for senior government managers). In 1980 and 1981, I helped him conduct seminars on influence for over one hundred managers.

In the mid-1980s, I designed a training module on influence for the Executive Leadership Program of the National Fire Academy, a facility for training fire chiefs and senior managers of fire departments. I have taught that module at the Fire Academy and elsewhere to over a thousand managers. It is always a winner!

Managers always find the approach extremely helpful. I say that not so much because of how they react to what I tell them, but because of the stories I hear them tell one another. During these training seminars, I ask them to apply the concepts by reflecting on their past experiences and by developing influence plans to deal with real situations in the present and future. The stories are fascinating, and their ability to use these tools, on such short acquaintance, is impressive.

You, too, will be surprised by how quickly you can grasp these ideas and apply them. Your personal and professional effectiveness will grow.

SECTION I

Overview

"Men are never so likely to settle a question rightly
as when they discuss it freely."

Lord Macaulay
Southey's Colloquies on Society (1830)

"The best victory is when the opponent surrenders
of its own accord before there is any hostilities . . . it
is best to win without fighting."

Sun-Tzu
The Art of War

"Perseverance is more prevailing than violence; and
many things which cannot be overcome when they are
together, yield themselves when taken little by little."

Plutarch
Lives, Sertorius Sec. 16

Chapter One

Overview and Roadmap

The Agile Manager returned to the office after his first meeting with the senior managers. He'd just been named plant manager and told either to fix the plant's problem in controlling costs or to get it ready for a quick sale.

He sat, looking out the window, reflecting. "I've been here before, and it's always the same. Let's see now. This is the fourth time in fifteen years I've been sent in to troubleshoot a plant. Good staff here, at least. But they are not going to be receptive to the kind of changes I'm sure we'll need. And they liked my predecessor a lot, which doesn't help. He was a nice guy, but he didn't push them on budgets. Fired for it, too."

The people at the meeting had been courteous, but they hadn't smiled much. As he was thinking about them, the Agile Manager took out a yellow legal pad and began making notes:

Ellen Taylor, marketing director. Young, but she's already a name in her field. She's smart, inventive, and assertive. She'll fight me hard on cost cuts. And headquarters thinks she's a star.

Tom Elliot, R&D director. Older, all kinds of prizes in physics. Expects deferential treatment. Technically superb, but he has no clue about money. He'll present a big education problem.

Carl Sims, production director. Maybe the most receptive to reducing costs. I'll have to sell him on my plan, but I sense he knows something has to be done.

Jane Wilson, secretary. Loved my predecessor. Treats me as if I myself had him fired. She could help a lot if I could win her over.

He tilted back in his chair. "These four look like the place to start," he thought. "If I can get them to buy in, it'll grease the skids for the kind of changes we need. But I'll have to think hard about which strategies to use with each."

Negotiation is the overall process of seeking agreement when two people have different goals or conflicting approaches to achieving goals. We face negotiation any time we want something from any of the people in our lives: bosses, subordinates, peers, clients, suppliers, competitors, friends, spouses, parents, or children.

We negotiate over all sorts of things: salaries, job assignments, perks, program initiatives, prices, priorities, career decisions, performance standards, and family matters. We do it to get our way, or at least to get a solution we can live with.

Often we are not very systematic in the way we negotiate. We wing it. That's probably OK in many situations, when the task is not too difficult or the outcome is not critical. However, when we have a difficult person to deal with, a tough issue to resolve, and we care a lot about the outcome—then we need to get serious. We need a plan, and we need a system to help us negotiate.

This book provides that system. It's a clearly defined process with specific action steps. It doesn't guarantee success—nothing can. But using the system will increase the probability of success. It will give you an edge when you most need it.

Observe the Flow of the Negotiation Process

The diagram on page 11 indicates the flow of the process.

1. Clarify Your Purpose. First, you need to identify your

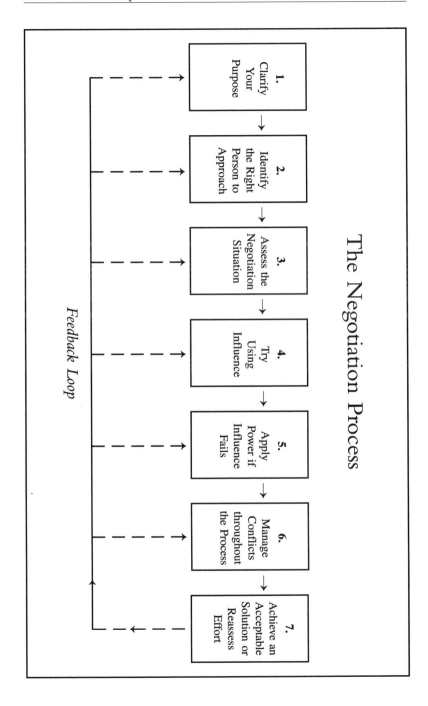

The Negotiation Process

1. Clarify Your Purpose

2. Identify the Right Person to Approach

3. Assess the Negotiation Situation

4. Try Using Influence

5. Apply Power if Influence Fails

6. Manage Conflicts throughout the Process

7. Achieve an Acceptable Solution or Reassess Effort

Feedback Loop

ideal outcome, what you'd most like to happen in this situation. There will be time later to think about possible compromises, but at the start it helps to establish optimum objectives.

2. Identify the Right Person to Approach/Persuade. Often your target is obvious. But sometimes it's best to first approach someone other than the person you ultimately wish to persuade. This step simply forces you to make a conscious effort to pick the right target person.

Use influence before you use power. It builds relationships and a commitment to the solution.

3. Assess the Negotiation Situation. Here you consider such things as the exact nature of the disagreement, your op-ponent's characteristics, your past history and relative power positions, and possible common ground for acceptable (not opti-mum) solutions. At this step you also ask questions like: What happens if I win? What happens if I lose? The answers to these two questions are important because they may persuade you to avoid negotiating, or to do it later.

4. Try Using Influence. Influence is a soft approach in which you try to educate the other person. You should always attempt it first. If successful, it builds both personal relationships and commitment to the solution. Even if it fails, it still helps pre-serve a good relationship when you use stronger tactics later.

5. Apply Power if Influence Fails. You may have to use power, a tougher approach, if your efforts at influencing have failed and you must move your project forward.

6. Manage Conflicts. Throughout the process, you'll encoun-ter differences in viewpoint. You'll need to address these as they occur.

7. Achieve an Acceptable Solution. If all goes well, you will arrive at an acceptable solution that both parties can live with. If that doesn't happen (note the feedback loop), you may need to rethink the various steps and repeat all or parts of the process. Note that the feedback loop can redirect you to any point in the process. However, it is always wise to rethink all steps (1-6) to better choose the most appropriate action. For example:

—Maybe you went to the wrong person.

—Maybe you did not use influence fully.

—Maybe you antagonized your target by using power too quickly or inappropriately.

—Maybe you left conflict issues unresolved during the process.

The feedback loop simply reminds you to critique your effort; to see where you may have gone wrong; and to rethink, revise, redo—until you get it right.

Roadmap of the Book

Knowing how the book is organized will help you use it. Keep in mind:

■ The book follows the flow of the negotiation process described in the model.

■ In each area (Negotiation, Influence, Power, and Conflict Management), I discuss general concepts first, then devote a chapter to specific tools and techniques.

■ All the tools are summarized at the end of the book for your convenience.

To help you understand the ideas, each chapter is introduced by a fictitious Agile Manager story focused on the ideas in that chapter. Within each chapter you will also find many stories from my own experience to help bring the concepts to life.

The book is designed so you can tap into any chapter that you might need and find valuable information. However, I'd recommend reading through the entire book once, to understand the whole process. And I'd also encourage you to try your hand at the tools and techniques as you read along. Opportunities to influence people occur daily, so you'll have no problem finding ways to apply the tools.

The Agile Manager's Checklist

✔ Recognize that persuading others is vital to your effectiveness.

✔ See negotiation as the process of persuading.

✔ Clarify your purpose at the start.

✔ Use influence—the soft approach—first.

✔ Use power if influence fails.

✔ Manage conflict as you go.

✔ Never give up. Try, try again!

SECTION II

Negotiation

"With reasonable men I will reason; with humane men I will plead; but to tyrants I will give no quarter, nor waste arguments where they will certainly be lost."

WILLIAM LLOYD GARRISON
WILLIAM LLOYD GARRISON, VOL. I
BY W. P. AND F. J. T. GARRISON

"In the long run men hit only what they aim at."

HENRY DAVID THOREAU
WALDEN

"If you don't know where you're going, you will probably end up somewhere else."

LAURENCE J. PETER
THE PETER PRINCIPLE

Chapter Three

Assess The Negotiation Situation

The Agile Manager got into his office bright and early and started planning.

"I've got three tough managers to bring aboard the cost-control program," he thought. "Taylor, Elliot, and Sims. Big persuasion job. I think Carl Sims is the place to start."

He glanced out the window. "Taylor and Elliot will fight the hardest. Best to warm up with Sims. He's not as old as Elliot, but he's been here the longest. Everyone likes and respects him. If I can get him on my side, it'll probably help with the others. And I think he knows cost cuts are necessary—he'll probably just fight about how much."

The Agile Manager stood up and started to pace. "He's easygoing and seems to listen. I think he knows I'm sincere. He also knows I have a tough job. He'll be willing to make some compromises we can both live with."

He paused a moment, then resumed pacing. "Even if the talk doesn't go well, he's not the type to spread a lot of stories that will make my task more difficult as I approach the others. Besides, he's smart and knows the organization well. He'll help me clean up my act."

The Agile Manager sat down again. "Yep. He's the place to start."

This book is mainly a tool kit to assist in building negotiation plans. The suggested process: Try to use influence (builds relationships and commitment), use power if influence fails, and manage conflict throughout the process. Later chapters specify how to do all these things. This chapter focuses on the question of whether or not to negotiate. Should we do it now, with this person?

B̲est T̲ip

Take time to identify the issue clearly and assess its priority. If the stakes aren't worth it, don't waste your time.

Before developing an influence plan, you'll need to examine the general negotiation situation—the problem or issue you'd like to press, the negotiation climate, and your opponent. You'll also need to assess the opportunity for negotiation: whether it's appropriate, your chances of success, and the effect of either winning or losing.

First Assess Whether to Negotiate

Here are ten factors to consider in assessing whether to negotiate:

1. *Nature of the Disagreement or Issue at Hand.* What's the fight about? Some problems are easy to identify; others are ambiguous and seem to defy clear description. But you must try to clarify the facts and the exact points of dispute. And don't neglect those issues where there is no known disagreement—to negotiate them effectively you need the same degree of clarity.

2. *Level of Conflict.* How intense is this fight? Are we respectfully disagreeing? Is there anger involved? If the solution can wait a bit, delaying negotiation can sometimes defuse a tense situation. That makes it more manageable.

3. *Priority of the Issue.* How important is this issue? How does it compare in importance with other things this person and I need to negotiate? Given its relative importance, should this matter be negotiated now? Could addressing it first handicap discussion of other important issues? Could it have an unfavorable impact on our relationship?

4. *Characteristics of Your Opponent.* One important pre-step is to be sure you are dealing with the right person. Normally that's the person with decision authority over the issue. But sometimes it is necessary or advantageous to approach an intermediary first. Once you identify the right target person, ask, "What's this person like?"

- Typically adversarial or friendly?
- Trusting or distrusting of others?
- Trustworthy personally?
- Willing to listen?
- Tolerant or intolerant of disagreement?
- Conscious and caring about the needs of others?
- Controlling or collaborative?
- Willing to compromise when occasion demands?
- Creative in developing solutions to complex problems?

The bottom-line question is: Are you dealing with someone likely to settle for something less than his or her optimum solution?

5. *Relative Power Position.* Power differences may mean little with parties of good will, but they can be decisive if one party chooses to play the power game. So you need to look at two things: the actual power position of you both and the willingness of either of you to use that power.

Past experience with your opponent is the best guide on this. The experience others have had with this person can also be useful, but it's not always reliable. That's because the use of power depends on the relationship.

6. *Status and Importance of the Relationship.* A history of good relations makes any negotiation easier. Even if the situation is serious, a past history of solving problems collaboratively indicates that negotiation is feasible. Consider, too, the future. Ask yourself, "What will be our future contact? How important will this relationship be?" In the rush to solve problems, you can damage relationships. A negotiation that could hurt an important relationship might best be deferred or avoided altogether.

7. Objectives. Here you clarify your expectations in a search for common ground. What is your ideal solution? What would you settle for? What do you think is your opponent's ideal solution? What might he or she settle for? Is there an area of overlap where you might agree?

Predicting an opponent's objective can be tough. We are often blinded by our own goals and values. You have to think like your opponent. Put yourself in her shoes. Consider not only her possible view of the problem, but potential ego needs as well. One helpful technique is to brainstorm with others, thereby discussing your thinking with people of sharply different perspectives.

> **Best Tip**
>
> Recognize that sometimes it's more important to preserve a relationship than it is to prevail in a conflict situation.

8. Opportunity for Creative Solutions. The "fixed pie" syndrome—assuming that one person's win is another's loss—inhibits creative solutions. Finding win-win solutions to really tough problems requires you to escape the boundaries of conventional thinking. You need to ask yourself challenging questions. What rules are standing in the way of innovative options? What resource constraints are you anticipating? Is time an issue? New, creative solutions can change the whole climate of negotiation—and they normally exist if you free your mind to see them. Consider breaking existing rules, finding additional resources, starting later, or asking for more implementation time. Make a bigger pie—and present that to your opponent for consideration.

9. Impact of Losing. What happens if you negotiate and lose? Maybe nothing, but this question deserves consideration. If losing could cause a loss of professional standing within your organization, handicap your ability to lead people, or hurt an important established relationship—then maybe you ought to back off and not press the issue further.

10. *Impact of Winning.* What happens if you win? Winning could have a big downside. Suppose that winning something from your boss is likely to cause your peers to view you with suspicion or even anger. Winning might not be worth the long-run costs in damaged peer relations. Again, backing away without negotiating might be the wisest decision.

Conditions That Favor Negotiation: A Checklist

Here is a checklist to use as a tool in making a decision on whether to conduct a negotiation. These conditions favor negotiation:

- ✔ Clarity about the facts of the disagreement.
- ✔ A bearable level of conflict.
- ✔ The issue is of sufficient priority.
- ✔ Opponent is:
    - Normally not adversarial
    - Trusting
    - Trustworthy
    - Willing to listen
    - Tolerant of disagreement
    - Conscious and caring of others' needs
    - Collaborative
    - Willing to compromise
    - Creative in developing solutions
- ✔ No power obstacle
- ✔ History of good relations
- ✔ Reasonable possibility of a mutually acceptable solution
- ✔ Creative solutions exist
- ✔ Losing won't result in unacceptable consequences
- ✔ Winning probably won't result in unintended bad consequences

When examining the considerations and conditions for negotiation, remember: There are no guarantees. You are just being careful by seeking a go/no-go signal to proceed. All factors will rarely be favorable. In the end it is a leap in the dark. But, as the great hockey player, Wayne Gretzky, has said: "You miss 100 percent of the shots you never take."

TWO EXAMPLES

To help you apply these tools, I'll relate two personal experiences. In one, I decided to negotiate. In the other, I decided not to. I'll describe the general situations and show how I thought my way to decisions.

Case #1: A Decision to Negotiate

During the 1980s, I was chair of the Business and Economics Department at my college. Early in that period we had twelve faculty serving about five hundred students (roughly 40 percent of the college's enrollment). We were one of thirteen academic departments reporting to the provost.

The president had instituted a merit pay system for faculty. The provost, though questioning this particular system, had the task of administering it.

Department chairs had to meet annually with the Provost to recommend merit raises for their faculty members. The first time I did this, the established merit increase had to be between 0 and 10 percent. The provost had been directed by the president to hold the average raise to 5 percent for the approximately seventy faculty members at the college.

I approached my task feeling I had to get my department average above the 5 percent college average. My faculty members expected this. Their class and advising loads far exceeded those of faculty in other departments. From their perspective, we were "carrying most of the wood"—bringing in a disproportionate share of the institution's revenue. They expected to be rewarded.

From the provost's perspective, we did not deserve special treatment. College norms and standards judged faculty by three criteria: teaching, scholarship, and service to the college community. While it was true we were doing more teaching than professors in other departments and doing our share of committee work, our level of scholarship was below average and few of our faculty held doctorates (which was then required for tenure and promotion).

My first problem was to decide whether to let nature take its course and settle for a below-average merit raise, or to negotiate vigorously. My thought process, keyed to the ten considerations in this chapter, was as follows:

Nature of the Disagreement or Issue: It was about money and the criteria for getting an above-average raise. We both understood that.

Level of Conflict: It would be a bit of a fight. It wouldn't be nasty; it never was with this provost. But he had his job to do—come in at 5 percent. And he had his own criteria for judging faculty, which went beyond teaching loads.

Best Tip

Think it all out: If losing could end in disaster, maybe it's best not to try. Similarly, winning can have a downside.

Priority of the Issue: This was a serious, high-priority issue. Salaries were low to begin with. My faculty felt unappreciated. I needed to win this fight.

Characteristics of the Provost: I could not have had a better person with whom to negotiate. He was:

-Always friendly to me.

-Trusting.

-Totally honest.

-A good listener.

-Tolerant of disagreement. He accepted it as a normal part of his job.

-Understanding of my needs—and he shared my concern for faculty morale.

-Typically collaborative.

-Often willing to compromise.

-Innovative in finding creative solutions to tough problems.

Relative Power: He had the power. He could do whatever he

wanted. But that was not his way. My experience with him was that he never played his power hand.

Status and Importance of the Relationship: Our relationship was excellent. We liked and respected one another. Maintaining this relationship was important to me. I needed that good relationship to lead my department effectively. Plus, I genuinely liked the provost.

Objectives: I felt the provost honestly considered my department faculty a bit below average from the perspective of the total criteria for merit (teaching, scholarship, and service). Given that, I expected him to want our average to be slightly below 5 percent. I knew I couldn't get much above 5 percent—but I wanted to get at least slightly over that mark. Overall, I felt I had a fair chance of getting what I wanted, but I knew it would not be easy.

> **Best Tip**
>
> Don't fear risk too much. Remember: Nothing gambled, nothing gained.

Opportunity for Creative Solutions: There was not a lot that could be done by way of creative solutions. There were other rewards I might seek for my faculty, like travel money, summer research grants, or favorable class scheduling. These would all help morale and indicate institutional support. But this fight was about money, and only one kind of money: annual salaries. And winning or losing would be judged by the average salary negotiated.

Impact of Losing: Losing would mean a loss of face for me in the department. I'd won some battles in the past, and the faculty expected me to win this one. With regard to the provost, losing this battle to him would not damage our relationship. Life would go on between us. But overall, losing would not be a good outcome—it would make my job of leading the department more difficult.

Impact of Winning: There was no significant downside to my winning. I knew the provost. If he gave us an above-average raise, he would not do it grudgingly. He'd make the decision and move on to other matters. Some other departments might get angry, but they'd be angry at the provost, not at me—and he was good at handling that.

All things considered, I decided to negotiate vigorously for an above-average raise for the department. And I used some of the tools, discussed later in this book, to design specific arguments—with considerable success.

We got our raise that year. And this negotiation was made easier in subsequent years—the provost never forgot how important this was to me.

Case #2: A Decision to Avoid Negotiating

A number of times in my life, on taking a new job, my predecessor in that job moved up and became my boss. It normally worked out fine—but not always. Here I'll discuss a case where it caused me problems and confronted me with an interesting negotiation situation.

I had had a lot of experience in the organization, so I felt particularly well prepared for this assignment. I brought to the task new ideas and a lot of self-confidence. My personal philosophy on leaving a job was always to walk away and never look back, but I soon found that wasn't my boss's philosophy. My every move seemed to irritate him; his meddling more than irritated me. The question was, could I negotiate a better relationship and establish some boundaries within which I could operate comfortably?

As I considered the items in the checklist in this chapter, I came up with mostly negatives. I did not like my boss personally or respect him professionally; there was no mutual trust; he had the power and enjoyed using it; compromise or collaboration were foreign to him; and he wanted his way, always.

I considered trying to negotiate with his boss—a significantly more powerful figure whom I knew he respected and probably feared. Should I go to this person, discuss the situation and request his intervention? I knew if he had simply said to my boss,

"You're not running things there anymore. Get off Hook's back."—that would have definitely been the end of the meddling.

But I did not know this senior person well, and my limited contact with him did not inspire confidence that he would take my side in this. I worried that his mentoring relationship to my boss would be the overriding factor. He'd side with him, I'd lose, and (importantly) I'd be in a worse position for trying.

I decided not to negotiate. It was probably the right decision, though the situation continued to worsen until my boss left for another job.

The Agile Manager's Checklist

✔ Always take time to assess whether to attempt a negotiation.
✔ Think through these questions:
    What's the fight about?
    How intense is it?
    What priority?
    What kind of opponent?
    Any power obstacle?
    What's the relationship like; how important is that?
    What do I want?
    What will I settle for?
    What might my opponent want?
    What might he/she settle for?
    Any creative solution possible?
    Any downside to losing?
    Any downside to winning?
✔ Then—decide!

SECTION III

Influence

*"Leadership is the ability to get men to do what they
don't want to do and like it."*

HARRY S TRUMAN

"Force has no place where there is need of skill."

HERODOTUS
THE HISTORIES OF HERODOTUS

*"Keep strong, if possible. In any case, keep cool. Have
unlimited patience. Never corner an opponent, and always
assist him to save his face. Put yourself in his shoes—
so as to see things through his eyes.*

BASIL HENRY LIDDELL HART
DETERRENT OR DEFENSE, 1960

Understand
The Basics of Influence

"Carl Sims is sick today," said the Agile Manager's secretary, Jane. "He can't make the meeting today."

Darn, he thought. "Thanks," he said aloud. "By the way, Tad Supanik told me great things about you. I'm glad, because I'm going to need a lot of help in the next few weeks." Tad was her former boss. The mention of his name made her smile and soften a bit.

"He's a good man," she said. "I was sorry to see him go."

"He's already landed on his feet—got a job running a plant in Michigan," said the Agile Manager.

"I heard that, too. I'm happy for him. Were you called in to spiff up the plant so the company could sell it?"

The Agile Manager was taken aback. "Well . . . not exactly. I was told to get costs in line. If I can't do that, I think they'll probably sell it or shutter it."

"A lot of good people work here. I'd hate to see that happen."

The Agile Manager saw an opening. "Me, too. That's why I'm so happy to have someone of your caliber helping me out. I'm going to have to do some things that will make certain people unhappy. But everything I do will be in the interests of saving jobs *and keeping the plant open. We all have a common interest in that, don't we?"*

"We sure do," said Jane. "Too many people here are interested in their own areas and don't seem to care about . . ." Her voice trailed off as she thought better of what she was about to say.

The Agile Manager smiled as he entered his office. Bingo, he thought, my first ally.

Let's start the discussion of influence by viewing it in the context of the four tool areas of this book: negotiation, influence, power, and conflict management.

Negotiation is the overall process of dealing with another in trying to get your way.

Influence is a strategy to educate other people about your point of view and involve them in it so that, in the end, they want what you want.

Power is the ultimate capacity to get your way. Power depends on the other person's perception of your resources, which is affected by such things as job title, charisma, and reputation for expertise.

Conflict Management is the process of resolving differences in viewpoint among individuals. It may require compromise, accommodation, or a number of other strategies addressed later in the book.

Now let's look at influence in more detail.

I might be able to get you to do what I want for a variety of reasons. You might do it because you like me, or fear me, or perhaps because you credit me with some particular expertise. That's getting my way through power. But you may not really be convinced that my way is the right way.

Influence is much more subtle than power. Power is breaking down the door; influence is picking the lock. Sometimes we must break down the door, but it is always wise to try to pick the lock first.

Influence is getting others to want what you want. It's tough to do, but the tools here will help you.

The theory of influence is simple to grasp. It involves four process activities and three influence styles. To apply the theory to a particular situation in which you want to influence someone: Understand the process activities, use the three influence styles to develop arguments, and follow the prescribed step-by-step process (discussed in the next chapter) in designing the influence plan.

Know the Four Process Activities

1. Lobbying: In this activity, you identify all the bases that you must touch to get your objective accomplished. Who are all the people you need to talk to, and in what order should you approach them?

Think about it. Haven't you found it useful in approaching someone on a touchy subject to be able to say, "I talked with so-and-so first." Or perhaps you might have said at times: "I'm coming to you first on this; I haven't discussed it with anyone else." Well, that's what lobbying is about. It's determining all the bases you need to touch, and in which order.

Best Tip

Get others to want what you want. It beats trying to get them to do what you want.

2. Negotiating: This is the direct bargaining that takes place with each individual you target. Understanding the influence styles in the next section will help you come up with appropriate arguments. The step-by-step process tool (in the next chapter) then prepares you to meet with the other individual.

3. Networking: Sometimes you need a third party to assist you, perhaps due to special relationships or technical competencies. You might want to send someone better qualified through experience or special expertise to make certain contacts. You may need to gain access to certain people through key intermediaries. Or, you might want to take advantage of established relationships.

For example, I once had a young woman secretary who was

the niece of a person who was difficult for me to deal with. So when I had something to sell him, I'd often say to her, "Mary, see if you can sell this to Jim for me." She'd come back a winner every time.

4. Assessing Our Constituency: This is essentially vote counting—keeping track of the degree of support you have. If you were going to a meeting to get approval for an idea from a group of seven people, wouldn't it be nice to know in advance how many were on your side? That doesn't mean you should never raise an issue unless you know in advance you can win. There are occasions when you might want to raise an issue knowing you'll lose, especially when it's for the sake of a principle.

But I don't think you can build a successful career by fighting a lot of losing battles. So getting a sense of who is with you and who's opposed is a useful strategy. And the very process of meeting with people in advance pays off. Sometimes people will oppose you in open meetings because they resent being surprised. Or, maybe they have some technical concerns, things that could have been put to rest if you'd met with them in advance. Plus, talking to people gives you a chance to learn—to clean up your act.

> **Best Tip**
>
> Sort out all the players at the start—know who's in the game and, if possible, where they stand.

Know the Three Influence Styles

Your influence "styles" affect both the substance of your arguments and the way you present them. The styles at your disposal are: logic, common vision, and mutual persuasion. Knowing the styles will help you find specific, persuasive arguments that will work best on the person you want to influence. The styles point toward arguments that might not occur to you otherwise.

As you read about each style, reflect on your capacity or inclination to use it. If you find you don't use one or more of the styles, don't worry! You can will yourself to use all the styles once you become acquainted with them. And to be effective influencers, we must have command of them all.

1. **Logic:** In using this style, you rely heavily on offering logical arguments, presenting the facts and marshaling the evidence. It's all about getting the facts straight and doing the necessary cost/benefit analysis. You do your homework carefully and make sure to leave no stone unturned in presenting all the facts and in developing counterarguments to points likely to be raised by others.

Use logic arguments in every negotiation. And while you won't always use common vision arguments, they are important to many people.

Think about it. When someone comes to your office to influence you, and he does a good job with logic arguments, you feel, "He really did his homework." Doing your "homework" is important in any influence effort, because most people in our society place a high value on logical arguments.

2. **Common Vision:** Common vision arguments can also be factual and logical—but they have additional qualities. They appeal to the values and emotions of the other person, and often they convey excitement about the future.

When using this style, you think through the possible hopes, values, and aspirations of the other person. You try to identify and articulate a common or shared vision of what the future might be like if the other person does what you propose. And you think through that future for the individual, for others, and for the organization.

In using this style, you often base your strategy on appeals to the other person's emotions. You try to kindle excitement about a better future which the other person may value for himself, for others, or for the organization.

3. **Mutual Participation:** When using the mutual participa-

tion style, you engage in a dialogue with others. You draw them into the discussion to such a degree that, in the end, they want what you want because they helped to develop it.

In using mutual participation, you let others know that you value their contribution. You don't push a point of view, but draw out the other person. You don't rush decisions, but you let the other person know that there is plenty of time to explore one another's views.

Properly applied, this style builds real commitment to decisions. One caution: You can't use this style successfully unless you have some flexibility in your position. Say I try to influence you using this style. You make a suggestion, and I can't or won't accommodate you. You're not going to feel like you are a partner in developing the idea, so my effort at using the style won't work.

Two Examples

Two examples from my own experience illustrate the styles. They will, I hope, convince you that using the influence styles to tailor your argument to the person is useful.

COMMON VISION. Some years ago, a colleague and I were briefing the president of our college. We were trying to sell him on the idea of organizing a management development center to provide management consulting services in our region, which was expanding with many new businesses.

We presented all the facts: the opportunities for workshops and other services, the costs of such services, and what it would mean to the college in terms of profits. The factual/logical story was a good one, but the president was unconvinced. By nature he was a common vision person.

We finally persuaded him with this argument: "When we get this center operating, we'll have our business faculty in the boardrooms of many local businesses. People will recognize that faculty members who can do a good job with their senior managers must be doing a great job with students at the college.

The reputation of your institution will grow."

That was an appealing argument to the president because it spoke to his values and to his concerns about the future of his institution. The argument might not have been effective with another person, but our analysis of his personality indicated that he was a common vision person. And it worked!

MUTUAL PARTICIPATION. In our college, as at most others, faculty members undergo tenure review. At the six-year point in service, they must put together a history of their service, including evidence of scholarship, which is then reviewed by an elected body of their peers. That group decides, on the basis of the evidence, whether the faculty member should be tenured. Failure to get a favorable recommendation means you must leave the college.

Use mutual participation when you need to build trust and commitment. Let others know you value their contributions.

When I was chair of the business department, some of my faculty, who did a good deal of consulting, asked me to get a letter from our provost stating that, for business faculty, consulting work could be considered as scholarship for tenure purposes. The provost initially balked at the idea, saying that business faculty had to adhere to exactly the same rules as all other faculty. As I talked to him about the virtues of my faculty he softened—and finally said: "OK, you draft the letter you want me to send you, and I'll consider it."

As you might imagine, he didn't like the first draft. "Tips the world too much in your direction," he said. But over a period of a month he and I passed this letter back and forth, negotiating its various provisions.

It finally got signed. It wasn't exactly what I wanted, but the provost had moved far in our direction. This was a good example of the use of mutual participation. In the end we both believed in that letter because we both had a hand in developing it.

Save Influence Techniques for Special Occasions

Don't bother to use the influence techniques every time you meet with someone. Actually, I suspect that most of the time you will do what I do: forget all about the theory and just wing it! That's reasonable, most of the time.

However, my advice is this: When you have a really tough opponent, a difficult issue to resolve, and you care a lot about the outcome, use the influence strategies outlined here. They'll give you an edge.

The next chapter provides a specific, step-by-step process to assist you in sharpening that edge.

The Agile Manager's Checklist

✔ Think of influence as your first line of offense. Try it before resorting to harder lines.

✔ Be guided by the four influence process activities:
  Identify all the bases to touch—and the proper order.
  Prepare a detailed plan to meet one on one.
  Use others to help you as necessary.
  Keep track of who is with you and against you.

✔ Use the three influence styles to help you find arguments:
  Marshal the facts and the logical arguments.
  Appeal to others' values, emotions, and hopes for the future.
  Suggest working together to develop mutually satisfactory solutions.

✔ Aim for a solution all can commit to fully.

Chapter Four

Use Influence Tools

"How much?!"

The Agile Manager stared right into Sims's eyes and repeated himself. *"$6 million in the next six months."* Sims shuddered.

The Agile Manager continued. *"But think about what's at stake—hundreds of jobs, not to mention what you all have been building here for the last twenty-five years."*

Sims nodded. *"There's a lot of skill out there,"* he said, pointing to the shop floor. *"I'd hate to see it go to waste."*

"So would I," said the Agile Manager. *"And I hope I made my case as to why we need to cut costs. The best argument, in my mind, is that it costs us 10 percent more than our two top competitors to make and market the main product line. One thing I don't know, though, is just where to cut."*

Sims looked at his shoes. *"I know a few areas where we could cut,"* he said. *"One of 'em is a big one, too. But what about the others? All this can't come out of my budget."*

The Agile Manager knew he was talking about Taylor in marketing and Elliot in R&D. *"I know it. I'm working on them. If they know you're on board, it'll be easier for me—"*

"Go ahead and tell them," interrupted Sims. "I'll talk to them myself if you want me to. Cut costs or close the plant? Come on—the choice is clear." The Agile Manager smiled, but he detected that Sims wasn't finished, and he knew what was coming: a request for his support on some issue dear to Sims's heart.

"I know how we could keep costs down long term," Sims said. "I went to this seminar a while ago on installing a preventive maintenance program, and . . ."

This chapter provides ten questions to ask yourself in developing an influence plan. Derived from the influence process activities and styles described in the last chapter, these questions represent a tool for planning a successful encounter. First, I'll list and explain the questions. Then I'll give you a chance to apply the tool in two real-life cases.

1. Whom Do I Want to Influence?

This may seem like a trivial question, but influence efforts often fail because we don't put enough thought into developing a complete list of all the individuals we need to contact to achieve our objective.

In this first step, make that list, including any intermediaries with whom you must deal.

2. In What Order Should I Approach People?

You can stumble if you neglect this step. The order is important for several reasons:

- *Confidentiality.* Some people may feel it is important that you deal with them prior to carrying your message to others.
- *Credibility.* Some people may be favorably impressed by hearing the reactions of those you approached earlier.
- *Learning.* Some people are smart or have particular expertise or experience you could use. Approach them first. They will help you refine your arguments.

3. What Do I Want to Happen?

Here you need to get specific. What do you want to happen at the first meeting with this individual? Obviously, you have an overall long-term objective for the negotiation. But you may not be able to get there in one giant leap. You may need several meetings, each with intermediate objectives. This step says to focus on one meeting with one person, and to be clear about your objective.

Best Tip

Pick each target person with care, and know what you want from each meeting with them.

For example, with a difficult target person, or someone you expect to learn from, set an objective of informing him or her of your desires and getting a preliminary reaction. Plan to come back later to get support for your idea.

Pick your objectives with a great deal of care. Ask for enough to move your cause forward—but not so much that you fail to gain any foothold of support.

4. What's the Target Person Like?

In this step, identify the relevant characteristics of the other person. What do you know that could help you choose an influence style?

This takes thought, maybe even some research. If you know the person well, a good clue would be the kind of arguments you've seen him or her use on others. If you don't know the person, you may find it helpful to consult others who do. You may get precise clues or only a vague portrait to guide you. But regardless of the outcome, this step is always worth the effort—it clarifies the target.

5. What Influence Styles Should I Use?

At this point, you are not quite ready to state specific arguments, but rather to pick appropriate styles (logic, common vision, or mutual participation). The following thoughts can help:

- Always include sound logical arguments. No matter what else you do, or how strong your other arguments, having sound logical arguments will strengthen your case.
- Common vision arguments are essential if you know you are dealing with a visionary type of person or someone with strongly held values on the issue. Logic arguments alone are unlikely to carry the day.
- Consider using mutual participation when dealing with a person inclined to participate, and when you have the time and flexibility of purpose to use this style effectively.
- Using a balance of all styles is appropriate when you don't know the target person very well and can't get insights from others. In this case, play out your arguments slowly, allowing time to observe the person's reaction. Emphasize the type of arguments that seem to get the best response.

6. What Actual Arguments Should I Use?

This is where the rubber meets the road. With your selected influence styles as categories, craft specific arguments. Decide exactly what you will say to the other person, and the pace and order of those arguments.

Best Tip

Study opponents to find just the right arguments. Anticipate their counterarguments and have an answer for them.

Recall the case of the college president in the last chapter. He was a common vision person—and the argument that persuaded him to establish a management development center was not the logic argument of financial gain. It was that such a center would place his faculty in contact with regional organizations and enhance the reputation of the college (a common vision argument).

Note that we first analyzed the person and decided to use the common vision style. That led to the specific visionary argument. The style was a category that helped find the argument.

7. What Conflict Should I Expect?

The task here is to predict what the other person might say in response to your arguments. This is an easy step to overlook. After all, you know you have good arguments. You've laid out a good story.

You may not like to entertain the idea that there's any room for objection, but usually there is. Anticipating objections is a necessary step for full preparation. If you neglect to identify areas of disagreement, you won't be ready to deal with them.

8. How Should I Deal with the Conflict?

Conflict is just a difference in viewpoint between two people. And it's inevitable.

Conflict must be managed. You may want to press hard on some points and give no ground. On other matters, you may see room to compromise or even make major concessions. Later in the book, I'll offer a variety of ideas and strategies to help you make such choices and handle conflict.

9. What Meeting Arrangements Must I Make?

This step addresses a variety of administrative and even some strategic issues:

- *Where should the meeting be held?* If you're dealing with a senior person, it may be necessary to meet in that person's office. But consider all options, including neutral locations like conference rooms. Also, consider individual preferences and institutional norms.

- *When should we meet?* Sometimes scheduling is so difficult that you have no choice. But whenever you do have a choice, be deliberate. Think about the habits and characteristics of the target person. Is he or she easier to deal with early in the morning, at the end of the day, or after a noon workout? Thinking this out can give you an edge—maybe the deciding edge.

- *Is any pre-work necessary?* Ask yourself, should I pre-brief an assistant, submit a memo before the meeting, or bring a summary paper with me to the meeting? Again, knowing the target person is key to deciding such matters.
- *What visual aids or papers are necessary at the meeting? And will these work in the place where the meeting is to be held?* This may sound trivial, but there's nothing more awkward than arriving with charts or visuals that you can't use in the room. It can sour the whole meeting.

10. How Can I Polish My Act?

Here are two things that can put a sharp edge on any influence effort:

—Test your arguments on trusted peers. They will bring diverse skills and knowledge to bear—about the issue, the target person, and process of influencing. This is a great way to clean up the act.

—Practice, practice, practice. No matter how good your arguments, having a polished, seamless presentation improves your chances of success. By this point, you've put a lot of effort into developing the plan—it pays to refine the presentation technique.

APPLY THE INFLUENCE TOOL

The ideal way to apply the influence tool described here is to consider an actual situation in which you wish to influence someone—and plan the encounter by thinking through the ten questions. At the end of the book I'll suggest you do that.

But, for the moment, try critiquing two actual influence efforts.

The best way for me to help you experience an effort at influencing is to write it as a play so you can read the exact words of the individuals. These two examples, by the way, were designed and acted out in a seminar that I conducted at the Federal Executive Institute for a group of government managers.

For each case I'll give you the general situation, the dialogue between the two individuals, and some comments. After reading the

situation and dialogue—but before reading my comments—ask yourself these four questions:

1. What was the overall quality of this influence effort?

2. Why was the quality good or bad? What were the strengths and weaknesses of the effort?

3. What influence styles were used?

4. How could the influencer have done a better job?

Case #1

Situation: A senior division manager (Bill) in a federal government agency (Department of Energy) is asked by his boss (John, an Assistant Secretary) to nominate someone from his division for a ten-month Congressional internship. Bill submitted a memo to John nominating a woman, Cathy, but never got a response.

Several days later Bill met John in the hallway and asked about his decision. John said: "Sorry I failed to get back to you; I decided not to nominate anyone for this position." To this Bill replied: "I'd like to have a chance to talk to you about that sometime." John told him to stop by his office that afternoon.

The scene is John's office, where Bill will attempt his influence effort:

Bill: John, I'd like you to reconsider Cathy as the nominee for the Congressional internship.

John: I don't doubt she's a good nominee if that's what you're concerned about.

Bill: I'm glad you think she's OK. I'd like to see you move on her nomination. Let me explain why.

John: OK, fire away.

Bill: Well, first I think she's a very high-quality nominee. I think she would get the job if nominated. Also, this is a plum of a job. If she gets the job, it will enhance the prestige and visibility of the agency. Also, she'd be working on the Appropriations Subcommittee, which always gives us a lot of trouble when we're trying to get our programs and budgets approved. Having Cathy there could be a real advantage—in things like early warning of problems and the sensitivity of issues to various subcommittee members.

John: Go on, I'm listening.

Bill: Look, we have a month to respond on this nomination. What I'd like to propose is that you make your own assessment of her ability. When you call me for information, let me send Cathy up. See if you're not impressed with her. If you are, all I ask is that you reconsider.

John: Fine, let's do that. No matter how it turns out, I always like to see our people get a chance for greater visibility; and I'll keep an open mind. But I'm still concerned—not about Cathy—I'm sure she'd be great over there. But what has me worried is the workload in your division. Can you really spare her? What assurance can you give me that you can cover her position (with no extra help) while she's away?

Bill: We've already thought about that. Our people are so excited about the possibility of Cathy getting this nomination that I've had all kinds of volunteers to pick up parts of her work. I am sure I can work this out so nothing will slip.

John: OK, let's think more about it. I'll take a closer look at Cathy when you send her up to brief me. You develop a more detailed plan to cover her absence. In about three weeks let's meet again on this. I guarantee a decision will come out of that meeting.

Bill: Fine, I'll follow up and schedule that meeting with you.

Comments: Before you read my comments, answer the questions on page 43.

This case provides an excellent example of the common vision style. Planting your person in the enemy camp (in this case, putting Cathy on this difficult subcommittee) is a visionary act—and argument.

Sending Cathy up to brief John, so he can participate more fully in the decision to nominate her, is a classic case of the use of mutual participation. Bill is essentially saying: Don't nominate her just on my advice. Check her out and decide for yourself.

John's direction to Bill to plan for Cathy's absence is an illustration of the influencee suddenly becoming an influencer—and it illustrates the pervasive nature of influence. You may start a meeting not intending to influence someone, and suddenly you need these skills.

Overall, I consider this a very good influence effort.

Case #2

Situation: A senior federal government division chief (George) wants to get his boss (Ed), head of a directorate in the Department of Education, to approve an award recommendation for a woman (Carol) who has worked for the division less than a year. The situation is complicated by the fact that Ed typically seems to enjoy rejecting George's recommendations. This is very discouraging to George, who tries to deal with Ed in writing to avoid the awkward confrontations that often occur.

In this instance, George sent the recommendation to Ed, accompanied by a very short memo requesting approval. Ed returned the award the same day with one word written on the memo: Denied. George became angry over this, and he scheduled a meeting with Ed. The scene is Ed's office. George is there with the award recommendation in hand:

Ed: What can I do for you, George?

George: I think you are being very unfair by denying this award.

Ed: What award?

George: Carol's.

Ed: Oh, that. I just don't think she deserves to be singled out for a special award—she hasn't even been here a year.

George: True, but look at the job she's done.

Ed: What's that?

George: I told you I was giving her your pet project—designing our new directive system. She did it, and did a great job.

Ed: OK, but isn't that what we hired her for? Are we going to give her a special award just for doing her job?

George: I'd say for doing it exceptionally well.

Ed: How well is that?

George: You know what I mean.

Ed: No George, I don't. How do you justify this award to all the other good people you have, doing equally good work, and for a longer period of time—years actually?

George: They'll be happy for her, I think.

Ed: What makes you think that? Have you talked to others about this award? Is there some sort of groundswell at work for Carol—everyone wanting to give her special recognition?

George: They'll be OK with it.

Ed: How do you know, George?

George: I just know.

Ed: That's just not good enough, George.

George (discouraged): It never is.

Ed: What never is?

George: Nothing I ever ask for is easy to get.

Ed: I'm not here just to make things easy. Tell you what I'll do. You go back and fully document the story on Carol and have some informal chats with some of the opinion formers in your division. If you then think Carol's case has merit above all others, come back to me and I'll discuss it with you.

George (rising slowly and walking slowly to the door): OK, Ed. I'll see what I can do to convince you *(discouraged tone).*

Comments: First, please answer the questions on page 43.

Relationships affect how you approach influence attempts. So do past history and relative roles.

With an influencee who turns you down often, you have to do your homework in advance. You need strong logic arguments (at a minimum) to make your case. George had few. If appropriate, you need common vision arguments as well. George had none. He might have discussed the effect a reward has on overall morale, or how this award might spur Carol on to shine in other capacities for the good of the department. Further, with this boss it's clear you would need to get him more involved in the decision (mutual participation). George offered Ed no opportunities to participate.

Best Tip

Plan your encounters by practicing with friends. Practice your presentation, too, until it's seamless.

George also needs to stop playing the injured party with Ed. Some bosses (maybe Ed is one) seem to enjoy beating down someone who permits it and who so obviously gets discouraged by it.

What might be appropriate here is for George to develop a history of his dealings with Ed and confront him nicely but firmly on how difficult it is to manage under such treatment. For his part, Ed needs to take steps to empower George if he wants to make him an effective subordinate.

Overall, this was a poor attempt to influence.

The Agile Manager's Checklist

✔ Influence planning is not manipulative—it is just thorough preparation to persuade.

✔ Influence planning is a process. Think through the major steps:

    Who is my target?

    What do I want?

    What is my opponent like?

    What influence styles should I use?

    What arguments—under each style?

    What might he/she say in response?

    How will I deal with that conflict?

    Where and when should we meet?

    What do I need to do before meeting?

    Who can help me test and polish my approach?

✔ Practice, practice, practice.

✔ Play out the script in your mind—anticipate problems—be fully prepared.

✔ Practice some more.

✔ Know that if influence fails, all is not lost—there are tougher approaches.

Power

"Power is not revealed by striking hard and often, but by striking true."

HONORÉ DE BALZAC

"After this time I surpassed all others in authority, but I had no more power than the others who were also my colleagues in office."

AUGUSTUS CAESAR

"In everything one must consider the end."

JEAN DE LA FONTAINE
FABLES, BOOK III 1668, FABLE 5

Chapter Five

Understand
The Basics of Power

Tom Elliot, R&D director, tilted back in his chair with his arms folded across his chest as the Agile Manager spoke. He pursed his lips and seemed to want to rebut nearly every argument the Agile Manager used.

"It was R&D that built this division," said Elliot when he got his chance to speak. "And it's R&D that will pull it out of a rut—though I'm not sure we're in one." He looked at the Agile Manager defiantly.

"You've come up with some great product ideas for us," said the Agile Manager. And a lot of duds, he thought. "But what I'm trying to say is this: The plant is at risk of getting shut down. We need to cut costs and control them better in the future."

Hah, thought Elliot. This place'll never get shut down. We're too important. "And what I'm trying to say is this," he said aloud. "You cut R&D and you're cutting a major lifeline here. We can pull you out of trouble if you'll let us. Hell, I'm hoping you'll increase our budget so we can get the new line into production."

The Agile Manager was tiring of this. He said, "I agree that we should get it into production faster. I was wondering whether we could outsource some of the technical work—"

"What?!" said Elliot sitting bolt upright and turning crimson. "Why, it'd take months just to get people up to speed . . ."

51

As the meeting wore on, the Agile Manager realized that education wasn't working and wouldn't work. He'd have to use power. "OK," he said finally. "You have some good points. Let me think about them. Let's meet again tomorrow at ten."

Power is the ability to get your way; the capacity to ensure that your point of view dominates.

Power sometimes gets a bad rap. We often hear about "abuse of power"—and it does occur, too frequently. Many sexual harassment cases are examples of abuse of power. But power should not be thought of as a bad thing. It is essential for individual and organizational success.

To understand the importance of power, let's reflect on its role in leadership.

Leadership is often used interchangeably with the term management, but they are quite different. You might be able to manage well by being adept at bringing together a lot of good people and integrating their efforts. But leadership is a lot more than that. To lead, you have to want to take an organization someplace, carry it to higher ground. Or you may want to sell a new program or project to higher management. This means change, and being an effective agent of change.

To lead, you need two things:

- A vision of what you want to change, and why.
- The capacity to persuade others to move with you in new directions.

Getting others to move in your direction often requires power. Influence is always the preferred approach, but it doesn't always work. That's when power becomes the indispensable tool for moving forward.

Another term that sometimes gets confused with power is "authority." But they are not the same. Authority is the *right* to command. Power relates to the *ability* to command. It is quite possible to have been given the right to command, by virtue of title or position, but still not have the capacity to move people in the direction of our vision. To lead, you simply must have power and be skilled in its use.

Understand the Nature of Power

You won't always be able to get people to actually want what you want (influence). But to lead, you sometimes must get your way, especially in matters of importance. Power is the key to doing so. If you can't pick the lock, you sometimes must push hard on the door, hopefully without breaking it! Proper application is the key to the successful use of power.

One more key point: Power is a matter of organizational muscle. Importantly, it isn't the muscle you actually have, but the muscle others think you have. We'll see this in some examples that follow.

There are two kinds of power:

- *Position Power.* This kind of power causes people to give you your way because of your legitimate title (boss, father, mother, teacher) and the capacity to reward or punish that usually accompanies that title.

Remember: To lead you must persuade; to persuade you often need power.

- *Personal Power.* This kind of power causes people to give you your way because of how they perceive your expertise, your special information, your connection to others, or your charisma. Failing to understand personal power can cause you to significantly underestimate your own total power and the power of others in lesser positions.

Most of us have a keen, intuitive understanding of position power because we experience it every day. We frequently give others their way because of their titles; and often we get our way because of our titles.

Personal power is equally important. Consider these examples:

1. EXPERT POWER. Athletics is a good illustration of *expert power.* Why are coaches able to get athletes to put forth extraor-

dinary training efforts? To a large extent, coaches get compliance because athletes view them as experts. They are convinced that doing what the coach says will help them perform better.

This example also shows the temporary nature of personal power. Others give it to us, and they take it away if we prove unworthy. The unsuccessful athlete will begin to fight the coach on training matters.

I witnessed an excellent example of this phenomenon at the college where I work. For many years we had a dozen or so international athletes training on campus for the Olympic decathlon. Our outstanding track coach attracted these Olympians.

The school sits at the base of a mountain. At the top of that mountain is a religious shrine called The Grotto. The coach required the decathletes to "run Grottos" frequently. It worked for most, and they willingly gave the coach his way. They respected his expert power and felt they'd perform better if they followed his guidance.

But some athletes balked. They found running Grottos so tiring that they did not have the energy to practice the various decathlon events. They literally took away the coach's ability to get his way through expert power—by the simple act of negotiating a more acceptable training program.

2. CONNECTION POWER. Government provides many examples of *connection power*—power that comes through knowing people in a position to aid your efforts.

In a seminar I conducted for senior federal managers at the Federal Executive Institute, we used assessment instruments to determine the "power styles" of the participants.

Most ranked high in connection power. The reason is obvious. Managers rise to senior levels in the federal bureaucracy by selling their programs, by getting funding for their agencies. And how do the really successful ones do this? Connections. They develop a network of supporters on Capitol Hill—senators, representatives, and staffers friendly to their programs.

When they use those connections to get their programs approved, they are using connection power. When political parties change after a national election, federal bureaucrats often have to start all over again to build their network, their connection power. Those who rise to the top are adept at this task.

3. EXPERT POWER. In production/factory situations, *expert power* becomes an important resource to get one's way. In the early to mid-1980s I had the opportunity to work as a training consultant to the M & M Mars Corporation. In the course of that training I developed power profiles of about five hundred of its managers and supervisors. Expert power was overwhelmingly the principal type of power.

It makes sense. In a factory, people respect those with knowledge or expertise in getting things done with assembly lines. It's a natural setting for expert power.

Best Tip

Serve your followers well: People can take away your personal power in a heartbeat if you prove unworthy.

Kinds of Power Bases

With those few examples as backdrop, let's take a more detailed look at the six bases (or sources) of power.

1. Legitimate Power: Positions in a formal hierarchy carry with them varying degrees of legitimacy to exercise authority. Subordinates give bosses their way, at least in part out of respect for their titles. Thus, legitimate power is the capacity to get your way that comes from your relative position in the organization.

2. Reward Power: Reward power refers to things a leader can do to motivate people to accept orders. It includes the ability to grant material rewards, such as pay, bonuses, and promotions, or nonmaterial rewards such as public praise.

3. Coercive Power: Coercive power is the ability to impose various forms of sanctions and penalties on people who fail to accept orders. In some respects this is a habit of mind and represents the negative alternative to reward power. With reward power, the issue is what is to be done *for* a person who cooperates. With coercive power, it is a question of what is to be done *to* a person who fails to cooperate.

4. Expert Power: Considerable research has revealed that people will follow others regarded as having a superior level of knowledge, judgment, or experience relevant to a particular situation. We just saw that in the examples of athletics and factories.

We also see examples in many emergency situations in which natural leaders arise spontaneously because people are ready to follow the person who seems to know what to do.

Relevance is critical in exercising this kind of power. An expert in weather forecasting would have no status as an infantry platoon leader. Similarly, a highly expert attorney is not likely to find this base useful as a manager. But when it exists, expertise is a powerful force, and the lack of it can turn things sour.

Best Tip

Maintain good connections with people. It's a way of tapping into their power.

During the Vietnam War, for example, many officers were placed in command positions simply because they had been successful in positions of responsibility in peacetime situations. Frequently, this did not translate to expertise at combat command. They had to be relieved, because their subordinates did not respect their expertise. Lives depended on knowing what to do, and they were unable to inspire that confidence in others.

5. Referent Power: This power source is one of the more difficult to explain. It encompasses all the personal attributes that tend to create followership—the person is attractive, nice, and dynamic. A person might also be a career model for others (intelligent, ethical, professional) and, therefore, likely to attract others. Charisma is often considered synonymous with referent power.

6. Connection Power: Connection power is derived from our linkage to others who may have any or all of the various forms of power. Think about it. Don't others sometimes give you your way because of such linkages?

Remember the senior federal government managers with connections on Capitol Hill. Staff people and secretaries often have connection power by virtue of their relationship to their bosses. Connection power is a way of tapping into the power of others.

Examples of Power

To illustrate the use of power, two stories might help:

The Naval Officer. During the 1980s, I regularly taught a seminar on power and influence in the graduate business program at Johns Hopkins University. At the conclusion of this class, I asked students to write a paper describing how they were going to use power or influence to get their way in some professional setting.

One student was a young woman, a Naval officer, and graduate of the Naval Academy at Annapolis. In her paper, she wrote that she was, at the time, on the faculty at the Academy. She also wrote that she had completed four years as an officer, that she had one more year to serve to complete her mandatory five-year service commitment, that she had decided to leave the Navy after that year was completed, and that she had so informed the Navy.

She wrote that she would like to persuade the commandant of the Naval Academy to place her on a committee being formed to recommend measures to improve the life of women midshipmen. She wrote, "I think I may have a great liability. Here I am, an Academy graduate, who has decided to leave the Navy. The commandant will probably think I'd be a bad influence on this committee. But I also have some definite power leverage. My father is an active duty four-star admiral, and four-star admirals have a lot to say about the promotion of two stars (like the commandant). Now, I'd never say anything bad about the commandant to my father, but the commandant doesn't know that!"

The moral of this story is that this woman understood power (her connection power to her father) and its potential to get her on the committee. Note too that it is not what she *would* do that was a threat to the Commandant—it was his possible perception of what she *could* do. I don't know if she got on the committee, but I do know she understood power!

4077 MASH. Good examples of power can be found in the old long-running television program *MASH*. The setting is, of course, a medical field hospital during the Korean War.

The characters provide excellent examples of several power bases. The commander, Colonel Sherman Potter, has the authority (right to command) by virtue of his office. That office, and the title of commander, also provide him with some capacity to command through position power (legitimate, reward, coercive).

But Potter has more than simply position power. He has a vast amount of personal power. An experienced soldier and surgeon, his people recognize his expert power; a nice person, he enjoys referent power; and, as a long-serving soldier he has extensive connection power with senior officers at headquarters.

Also, Potter is smart enough to know he doesn't possess all the power in the unit. Captain Hawkeye Pierce, a skilled surgeon and personal friend to everyone, can get things done through both expert power and referent power. And Corporal Radar O'Reilly, the company clerk, is respected for his expert power—he knows how to do many things, from getting scarce supplies to contacting your wife in New York from a field telephone in Korea.

The Agile Manager's Checklist

✔ Power is the ability to get your way.
✔ Your power depends on others' perception of your resources, not your actual resources.
✔ Know the two kinds of power:
   Position Power, which gets you your way because people respect your title or position.
   Personal Power, which gets you your way because people respect your personal qualities.
✔ Know your power bases. Know why people give you your way.

Chapter Six

Use Power Tools

The Agile Manager could hear Tom Elliot in the outer office bantering with Jane. *I'm no expert in R&D, he thought, so it's pointless to try to assume any expert power. But I think Elliot knows I have some knowledge that bears on the financial situation here. He'll listen to that.*

"Come on in, Tom," said the Agile Manager when he heard a knock on the door. "Beautiful day out, isn't it?"

"Wouldn't know," said Elliot jovially. "I was here all night working." Elliot smiled broadly.

"Well, you kept me up late last night thinking," said the Agile Manager, smiling back. "You had a lot of good arguments for keeping R&D fully funded. Unfortunately, I don't have time to go over each one point by point. I'm expecting a conference call with headquarters any minute. But let me share a piece of information with you." Elliot looked at him intently.

The Agile Manager continued. "This division's R&D work has always been done at this plant. But headquarters thinks R&D is one of the undisciplined spenders here. If I can't get costs in line—and before they close the plant—they'll close down our R&D facility completely and get the work done elsewhere." Elliot blanched. "That's why I'm pressuring you. Tom, this is serious. I need your help."

"That's bad news," said Elliot, trying to sound calm. "Can I have some time to think about this"
"You bet," said the Agile Manager as he ushered Elliot out the door. I've got him, he thought. He'll never agree that it's right to cut R&D. But he doesn't want to lose his status as Mr. Corporate R&D. He'll come back in a different mood, I'm sure.

This chapter provides a ten-step process as a tool for using power. It assumes that you've tried the softer approach (influence) and failed. This tool uses the concepts of power described in the last chapter. It blends them into a series of questions you address to develop your plan to use power. Here are the questions:

1. What Are My Objectives?

Having failed to achieve your influence objective, you may want to change objectives when you use power. It is important to revisit the objectives and be clear about them.

- *Substance Objectives:* What do you want regarding the project or proposal?
- *Relationship Objectives:* What do you want the relationship to be after using power?

Power can be tough on relationships. If you want to maintain friendly relations, you might need to settle for less in the way of substance objectives.

2. Do I Need to Use Power Now?

This is another way of asking if your efforts at influencing have been exhausted. If you still have opportunities to influence, make another effort. Even if you decide that power is necessary, there is still the question of timing. Must you use your power right now, or will a cooling off period make it more acceptable?

3. What Power Bases Do I Have at My Disposal?

In this step, think of each power base relative to the individual you're trying to persuade. You have to decide which power bases will be effective with that person.

Honesty is important in this step. For example, you may feel you have expert power to help your case. But the real question is: Does the other person see you as having expert power? If not, you can't use that power base. Remember: Your power lies in the perception others have of your resources.

4. Is the Use of Power Permissible in My Organization?

In some organizations, the use of power is almost unthinkable. In others, it is quite acceptable. The issue is never simple, and we must be careful not to stereotype. Two examples may help:

Academic Institutions. Colleges typically are not friendly to the use of power, particularly on academic matters. Faculty members want to be consulted and have their views valued. But today's college costs have risen to the point that faculty values about academic content must often take second place to economic considerations. Presidents and boards of trustees increasingly recognize that they simply must use power to change programs in the interest of fiscal survival.

The Military. Perhaps your gut reaction is to think of the military as a place where power is accepted without question. I spent many years in the U.S. Army, and until recently accepted that stereotype. But last year a colleague of mine and I were asked to write an article on the culture of the military. This deep reflection revealed that the military has many cultures, some where power is acceptable, others hostile to the use of power.

For example, troop units in combat could not function without responding to power. However, not all power bases work in combat. Charisma (a form of referent power) always helps, and expert power is essential (troops need to know the leader "knows"). Legitimate power (being commander) is important. But it will not, alone, carry the day. In our paper, my colleague and I also looked at war colleges and Pentagon staffs—settings where power works less well.

In short, this step encourages you to assess the acceptability of power in the setting in which you work.

5. What's the Other Person Like?

Look for relevant characteristics that can help you select appropriate power bases. Certain kinds of power can alienate some people, so pick power bases with care.

For example, position power, particularly coercive power, is unacceptable when dealing with bright, creative people. They tend to respond better to expert power and referent power. Conversely, some people may only respond to coercive power.

6. What Is My Personal Relationship with the Other Person?

If you have an easy, friendly relationship with someone, the sudden use of power could be a terrible shock. It might cause the entire situation—and the relationship—to take a bad turn. Be sure to think about both the current status of the relationship and what you want it to be in the future.

7. What Power Bases Should I Use, and What Specific Arguments Should I Make?

As in the case of influence styles, the power styles become categories to help in developing specific arguments. Your assessment of your power bases and their acceptability in your organization, and with the individual involved, should lead you to specific styles—then to specific arguments.

For example:

- In using legitimate power, you might use the phrase: "As plant manager, I have to consider the future welfare of all the senior staff in making this decision."
- In using expert power, you might say: "The ten years I've spent in sales have convinced me we have to change what we are doing in that area."
- In using reward power, you might say: "I've got to believe that this transfer will help your long-term career prospects."

8. What Conflict Should I Expect? How Should I Deal with It?

The chapters on conflict will provide specific conflict-management tools. For now, just recognize the need to anticipate opposing views. You can't always be successful in predicting, but if you don't try, you are likely to be surprised by the reactions of the other person. The best advice is to do the best job possible to anticipate conflict areas, then try these ideas on trusted peers to refine your approach.

9. What Administrative Arrangements Should I Make?

It is sometimes said that the devil is in the details. The best strategic approach can fail for lack of attention to the administrative arrangements:

- Meeting time
- Meeting place
- Pre-meeting information furnished
- Visual aids
- Practice session with trusted peers

These are some of the matters to consider as part of a comprehensive plan to use power.

10. What Do I Do If Things Bog Down?

Remember, this is the final effort. Soft approaches have failed. If, in the course of the meeting, you sense that your use of power will fail, you need a next move. You never want to lose completely. Best to think out options in advance. For example, you might plan to suggest parting and scheduling another meeting later. This would give both of you an opportunity to reconsider positions and to develop new arguments. It can also help in situations in which people have gotten angry or emotional.

THE BOB KNOWLTON STORY

This is a great case study on power used in many business schools. Originally a written case, it was later adapted to film, and has recently been updated.* I'll summarize the story here, pose a few questions, and provide some thoughts on the case.

---

*The updated version of this film is now distributed by Video Publishing House, Inc., 930 N. National Parkway, Schaumburg, IL 60173-9920. 1-800-824-8889.

The Story: The story involves three people in a large high technology firm: Bob Knowlton, an engineering project manager with about eight technical people in his group; Catherine, Bob's boss; and Simon, an extremely talented engineer that Catherine has just hired away from another firm.

The story begins with Catherine dropping by Bob's office to tell him he'll soon have a visitor: Simon. Catherine says she wants Bob's advice on where to place Simon. Catherine then abruptly departs for a dinner meeting.

At about quitting time, Simon drops in on Bob. He seems so bright and inquisitive about everything Bob is doing that Bob becomes quite intimidated. When Simon keeps Bob well into the evening, Bob becomes angry.

The next morning, Catherine calls Bob in, tells him that she had breakfast with Simon and that she'd like to leave him in Bob's group for a while, pending a final assignment decision. Bob doesn't like this a bit. He would like to part company with Simon, but he seems afraid to tell Catherine. He consents to this temporary assignment.

> **Best Tip**
>
> Never lose by default. Always have a next step in mind if things don't go as planned.

Simon moves into Bob's group and Bob increasingly sees him as a threat. Bob's people turn more and more to Simon because he is so bright. Simon continually mentions lunches and breakfasts he has with Catherine. Bob becomes convinced that Catherine is planning to replace him with Simon.

Every time Bob meets with Catherine she asks how Simon is doing and if Bob is happy with him in the group. Bob, his fears now in control of him, never levels with Catherine, never says he'd like to get rid of Simon.

Things come to a head when Simon saves a project that Bob was ready to abandon, makes a great presentation to the board, and receives high praise from board members and Catherine. At a company party after the presentation, Bob finally musters up the nerve to confront Catherine, saying: "Catherine, I must talk to you." Catherine smiles pleasantly and says: "Sure Bob. Give me just a few minutes with Simon. There's something I want to talk to you about also."

This blows Bob's mind. He feels sure he's about to be replaced. He bolts from the room, later finds a new job in a different firm, and writes a short letter to Catherine thanking her for her friendship over the years. He says he's resigning for personal reasons, and recommends that Simon take over his group.

Catherine is astonished. It becomes apparent (from her reaction in the film) that she had deep respect and affection for Bob and had no intention of replacing him. She was honestly trying to get Bob's advice on where to place Simon.

Interpretation of the case: I've watched hundreds of managers wrestle with the issues in this case (it is my favorite case to use in training programs). Most feel Bob Knowlton is the main culprit—that he is a wimp for not confronting his boss on such a simple matter. To many, the case seems simple at first glance. But the power implications are profound. Consider the following questions:

What does Bob want from Catherine? He wants to get Simon out of his group.

Does Bob have the power to get his way in this matter? Yes, he does. It becomes apparent in the film that he has both expert power and connection power in Catherine's mind. She's not a very warm person, but she thinks Bob is a very bright guy, and that she and Bob have a good relationship. The problem is that Bob, overcome by his fears, does not know how Catherine feels about him. So one message in this case is that you can have power (the ability to get your way) but doubt your power resources and fail to use it.

Who's most at fault in this case? Well, Bob's a wimp, and Simon is an insensitive genius who doesn't have a clue about how to join a new group. But the main fault, in my view, is with Catherine. And it is a power issue as well.

Catherine is the boss. She gets paid to attract and retain good people. She thought Bob was a great person, but she let him get away.

What Catherine failed to do was *empower* Bob Knowlton. If

we have great people working for us we ought to let them know how we feel about them. Many times we don't, simply because we think they know—but often they don't. Think about this a moment. Haven't you at times had to deal with an authority figure (boss, coach, teacher, even maybe a parent), not knowing how that person felt about you? Personally I've been there a number of times—and I didn't always feel strong enough to ask.

The solution for Catherine, and for all of us when we play boss, is to empower our good people. Often the subordinate can't quite reach up to make the connection. But the boss can always reach down.

I feel Bob Knowlton would have been helped by the tools in this book. He might have first tried to put Simon in his place using his position power. If that failed, he could then have attempted to use the influence tool with Catherine.

Failing that, he could have used the ten steps of the power tool with her. It would have worked; she liked and respected him. It may seem like overkill to be so deliberate in designing a meeting to persuade—but better to make this effort than to lose a job you like.

The Agile Manager's Checklist

✔ Consider these questions before deciding to use power: What's my objective? Could using power hurt our relationship? Have I exhausted influence efforts? Do I have the necessary power? What type is it? Is using power OK? What type power might be most/least effective with this person? What specific arguments should I use? What conflict might occur? How would I deal with it?

✔ Attend to the administrative arrangements (meeting time, place, etc.). Failing to do so can spoil the effort.

✔ Think: What will I do if things bog down? Always have a next move.

Conflict Management

"He that wrestles with us strengthens our nerves and sharpens our skill. Our antagonist is our helper."

EDMUND BURKE
REFLECTIONS ON THE REVOLUTION IN FRANCE (1790)

"Chance favors only the prepared mind."

LOUIS PASTEUR

"All government—indeed, every human benefit and enjoyment, every virtue and every prudent act—is founded on compromise and barter."

EDMUND BURKE

Chapter Seven

Understand
The Basics of Conflict

The Agile Manager left the staff meeting angry at Ellen Taylor and at himself.

Taylor challenged him on an order he issued concerning one of their largest accounts. She had said, "I wish you'd consulted me on this. That's not how they like to do business. I know a better way . . ."

At that, the Agile Manager got mad. "We've turned the corner on this one, Ellen," he snarled. "We're committed. Let's move on."

The exchange dampened the meeting, and Taylor was sullen for the rest of it.

The Agile Manager felt silly and little depressed. "Whatever her faults," he thought, "that was no way to treat a bright, well-respected manager. And I can't afford to lose her entirely—I need her support here and she has the marketing and finance departments at headquarters behind her. It's also no way to handle conflict.

"I have to put this to rest now, even though I think she was looking for an opportunity to challenge me." He dialed the phone.

"Ellen? I'm sorry I . . ."

A difficulty we often have in dealing with conflict is that we don't distinguish between conflict and bad interpersonal relations.

- *Conflict* is simply a difference in viewpoint between two individuals over a given issue at a given point in time. The two individuals may actually like one another personally.
- *Bad interpersonal relations* means the two people dislike one another. Individuals may agree on the issues yet experience bad interpersonal relations.

Conflict can occur over turf issues, resources, rewards, and differences of opinion on technical issues. Conflict is inevitable between forceful and creative people. It is useful and necessary for creativity. So conflict is something to be encouraged, though it must be managed to be constructive. Bad interpersonal relations, on the other hand, are normally dysfunctional and should be avoided.

Let's consider how to manage conflict and avoid bad interpersonal relations.

Use This Framework to Manage Conflict

The grid on the opposite page will help you manage conflict. It's adapted from a similar one found in K. Thomas's "Conflict and Conflict Management," from the *Handbook of Industrial and Organizational Psychology*, edited by M. D. Dunnette. (New York: John Wiley & Sons, 1976), 90. Used with permission.

To come up with a strategy for dealing with conflict, select the appropriate conflict-management styles. You have five to choose from: competition, accommodation, compromise, avoidance, and collaboration.

As the grid shows, you can array these five styles on a set of axes. The horizontal axis represents our concern for our own goals: how much we care about getting our way (on this issue, at this time). The vertical axis represents our concern for the other person's goals: how much we care about the other person getting his or her way (on this issue, at this time).

Here's a brief explanation of each of the styles:

Competition. Use this style when you must get your way

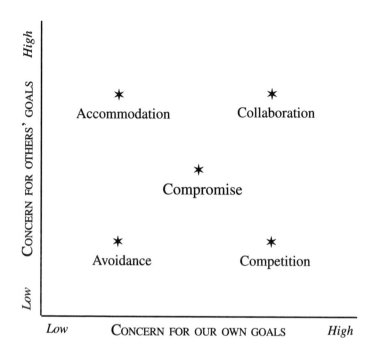

and do not care about others getting their way. Go to the mat; give no ground.

Accommodation. Use this style when you are willing to sacrifice your own interests to let others get their way. In return, you may want cooperation from them later. But at this time and on this issue you give ground.

Compromise. Use this style when you can afford to give others part of what they want and get only part of what you want. Sounds reasonable, and it often is. But it is hard to do if you are dealing with a person who likes to win all the time—and some people are like that.

Avoidance. Use this style when you want to suspend negotiations temporarily. No one gets their way at the moment. You'll resolve the conflict later.

For example, suppose that during a negotiation you encounter conflict. You realize the problem is a lack of critical information to make an informed decision. You might suggest suspending the negotiation until you can obtain the essential information. This is not damping out the conflict. You know it will have to be resolved eventually. You are merely saying that no one wins at this time.

Another example: You're dealing with an individual you don't get along with very well. You might defuse the bad interpersonal relations by saying: "This is really a tough problem and may take some work. Why don't we each appoint one of our people to work together on this? Maybe they can come up with a solution you and I can buy."

Collaboration. Use this style when both parties need to get their way fully. Take the example of two division chiefs trying to decide how the money allocated for a project should be split between their divisions. Let's assume they both become convinced of the other's need for significantly more funding than the project's budget will allow. Assume also that both divisions must participate for the project to succeed.

It's time to use the collaborative style. Maybe the two division chiefs need to go to senior management to recommend increased funding for the project.

Best Tip

Use a competitive style when you absolutely must get your way—no matter how it affects other people. Go to the mat; give no ground!

To use this style, you might have to take the lead and do a little educating. Use words like: "You've convinced me you need your money, and I hope I've convinced you I need mine. But there's not enough budget to meet both our needs. Let's go up the tape and ask for more budget on this. This project will fail unless we both get what we need."

Considering and selecting one of these five styles helps you manage conflict strategically. The framework also provides a lens to help you see the styles used by others. Last, it also highlights an important reality about conflict: We cannot win all the time. Sometimes you must give ground to others.

Avoid Bad Interpersonal Relations

Let's turn now to interpersonal relations. How can you keep your one-on-one relationships healthy and avoid the dysfunctional bad feelings that can occur when things get off track? Three approaches can be helpful:

1. Appreciate the other person as a multi-role person. Often we see people in a single, dominant role and forget they have many roles in their lives.

A woman friend of mine, a bank vice president, told a group of my students a story that illustrates this. She's had a rapid rise through the ranks at her bank.

Best Tip

Encourage conflict—but do your best to avoid bad interpersonal relations.

During much of that time she was married to another busy professional, but she had no children. One of the things that had made her so valuable to the bank was that she could be called upon anytime to make a sudden trip or fill in at the last minute at a dinner or meeting. For years it was no problem, and her reputation for flexibility soared.

Then she had two children in quick succession. She found herself having to decline when asked to make quick changes in personal plans to accommodate the bank. This caused strained relations with the bank's senior managers. They seemed irritated when she would turn down assignments. She didn't normally tell them exactly why she was unavailable because she thought they realized the impact of two children on her life.

This is an example of role conflict. It caused bad interpersonal relations because the bank hierarchy saw this woman only as a dynamic worker. They failed to see that she had other roles demanding attention. Once they all got together and discussed this problem, they did understand.

She was subsequently promoted to vice president, so it is a success story. But it might not have been so.

The lesson: Remember that others have roles you don't always know about. When they don't behave as you think they should, you should ask about the reason rather than have relationships deteriorate. You also occasionally need to inform others of your multiple roles. They might not think to ask.

2. Don't talk down to others. The opportunities for talking down are endless. You encounter them daily. You go to see the boss to explain the status of a project. The boss says (talking down): "Things look bad, and I think you haven't been paying enough attention to this project." You get angry and say (also talking down): "I don't think you have the technical background to make that kind of a judgment." The result is two people angry at one another, the breeding ground for bad interpersonal relations.

How can you prevent this? By cooling it when someone talks down to you. Shift the topic. But don't talk down in return. I'm not saying that we should never talk down to another person. Occasionally it's necessary to get someone's attention. But it should be possible to do it in a way that preserves the other person's dignity.

Further, if maintaining good interpersonal relations is an important objective, and normally it is, then you should not talk down, period. Theory helps here. It puts you in control, because it gives you the perspective to see what is happening and helps you avoid dysfunctional actions.

3. Make sure that both people have the same facts and share the same reality about the situation. We don't all have the same input on any given issue. We read different things, talk to different people, and have personal biases and intellectual differences in processing information. A first step in resolving any argument is to ensure there is agreement on the facts.

I experienced this when I was a group commander in the army. I had four battalions in my group and eight different battalion commanders working for me during an eighteen-month period. All the commanders were great, except one.

I had told them all the same thing initially: "This is a tough job; you'll be in trouble 20 percent of the time. If you can hold it at that, you'll be OK. And, if you ever get in real trouble with me, I'll let you know."

I thought that was pretty clear, and it did work well with seven of them. But the other one was a bit too laid back for my taste. He was smart, but he didn't find and deal with problems quickly enough. So I spent about 40 percent of my time on problems in his unit.

I'd go there often, find lots wrong—and he'd just smile and say something like, "OK, I'll fix it. Let's go to lunch." It drove me crazy. I kept thinking: I'm telling this guy he's in deep trouble and he just doesn't care.

Best Tip

Avoid talking down to others! If you must do so, find a way to let your opponents preserve their dignity.

But I now know that wasn't really true. He heard my words all right. But he chatted frequently with his fellow battalion commanders who assured him he was doing fine, and that they all had similar problems in their units. They meant well, but they caused him to hold a different view of the reality of the situation than I had.

- I felt: He's in a lot of trouble and I'm telling him so.
- His reality was: I'm not in any more trouble than the other commanders.

This difference in "reality" got me mad, and nearly got him fired. It was partly my fault. I should have seen what was happening and said: "Remember when I said I'd tell you if you got in real trouble with me? Well, you are!" I might have helped him professionally. At least, I'd have saved myself a lot of effort and aggravation.

The Agile Manager's Checklist

✔ Bad interpersonal relations mean bad blood between two people—try to avoid it!

✔ Conflict is just a difference in viewpoint between two people. It's useful, so encourage it.

✔ To avoid bad interpersonal relations, see others as multi-roled, don't talk down, and clarify the facts.

✔ To manage conflict, *compete* if you must win, *accommodate* if your opponent must win, *compromise* if some of what you want is enough, *avoid* to break an impasse, *collaborate* to build a bigger pie.

✔ Know you can't win all the time.

✔ Some people think they can win all the time. You may have to educate them.

Chapter Eight

Use
Conflict Management Tools

The Agile Manager finished reading Tom Elliot's memo. He smiled. *I guess he believed me, he thought. He's scared.* He glanced down at the line again. *". . . and so I think I can probably find ways to cut 20 percent, although it will be painful."*

We probably don't need a contribution quite that high from R&D, thought the Agile Manager. But I can use his offer to get him solidly behind me.

The Agile Manager walked down to R&D. He found Elliot in his office. "Tom," he said. "I read your memo. And I sincerely appreciate your work on this. It helps me a lot."

Elliot looked relieved. He hadn't been sure that figure was high enough and was afraid the Agile Manager would ask for more.

"I did the best I could," he said. "I'm hoping I don't have to lay anyone off, but that looks doubtful at this point."

"Well, I have some good news for you," said the Agile Manager. For now, let's think 10 percent instead of 20 percent. I'll try to hold it there. You're doing great R&D work, work that's important for the firm's future. We don't want to lose that."

"That's great!" said Elliot.

The Agile Manager was happy too—his compromise won him another ally.

Before using the tools of conflict management, you need to be sure you are dealing with conflict and not bad interpersonal relations. If bad relations exist, deal with that first— before conflict—and differently.

Indications of bad interpersonal relations include:

- You dislike the other person.
- The other person seems to dislike you.
- Each of you gets angry with one another over relatively unimportant things.

When those conditions exist, consider who's at fault. Realize that maybe it's you. Questions to ask include:

- Have you missed seeing some role conflict or failed to respect the other person's differences in personality or values?
- Have you talked down to the other person?
- Have you failed to consider that the other person may hold a different truth or reality about the situation, simply because he or she is traveling in different circles and thus gets different input?

Any of these factors can cause a person to seem obstinate or arrogant and cause bad interpersonal relations. Think these things out and take action to repair the relationship before addressing the conflict (which is, remember, a difference in technical views about some issue).

The conflict management tool or approach suggested here has three components:

- Five questions to consider.
- Five things to do prior to meeting.
- Five things to do at the meeting.

Consider These Questions

1. **What exactly do we disagree about?** It is essential to clearly identify the problem.

2. Why do we disagree?

- Do we disagree on the goals to be accomplished or just on the methods to achieve those goals?
- Do we both understand the situation similarly? Do we hold the same facts, make the same assumptions?
- Do we have the same facts, but react to them differently because our roles in the organization differ?

3. Have I exhausted efforts to educate (influence) the other person? Here it's important to rethink the influence effort—all the actions you took to provide facts, search for common ground, and develop solutions jointly. Be honest in this examination. If you have not made a full effort to persuade through influence, develop a new influence plan and try it.

4. Have I antagonized the other person through an inappropriate use of power? As we've seen, power is a good thing, and it's necessary if influence efforts fail. But used prematurely or in the wrong way it can spark bad interpersonal relations and conflict. Again, be honest with yourself. If you've made a mistake, act to improve the situation. Very often, simply acknowledging to the other person that you were heavy handed is all that's necessary.

Build good relations as a first step. They help immeasurably in managing conflict.

5. What's the other person like? You asked yourself this question earlier in the negotiation process. But ask it again if conflict occurs.

Look for relevant characteristics that provide clues as to which conflict management styles will be effective. These clues are best found in the prior behavior of people in conflict situations. If you know the person well, the style to use might be easy to identify. If not, you may need to discuss that person's characteristics with others.

Specifically, search for the conflict-management styles the other person typically uses.

- Does he or she always have to win?
- Does he or she compromise easily?
- Will he or she work in a collaborative way to find innovative solutions?
- Does he or she recognize the need to accommodate others at times?
- Would he or she likely be willing to suspend discussions temporarily if things bog down?

Answering these questions should help you pick an appropriate conflict-management style.

Do These Things Prior to Meeting

1. Request a meeting. An obvious action, but tone is important when conflict exists. Ask for the meeting in a nice way. Mention that you care a lot about the issue, that you know the other person does too, and (importantly) that you feel sure things can be worked out. The climate of the meeting is affected by how you request scheduling one.

2. Be candid about the reason for the meeting. An approach might be: "We have some significant areas of disagreement on this. I'd like to get it resolved in a way that meets both our needs. I know you would, too."

Best Tip

Seek to understand the nature of the conflict. You can't solve until you see.

3. Lay cards on the table. Consider sending a memo or short "point paper" prior to the meeting. It indicates good will. The other person knows you are not going for a preemptive first strike. The paper can restate facts, and thereby extend your influence effort. It can also clarify what you want and may help the other person see possible areas of agreement.

Many people disagree with this approach. Some feel it's a mistake to tip your hand in advance. I think, however, that it generates good will and tends to defuse the conflict atmosphere.

4. Educate the other person on the conflict management styles. The previous step educates the other person on the substance of the issue. But a memo can also educate him or her on the process.

You now know about the five conflict management styles. Chances are, the other person does not. Just a casual mention of some conflict resolution possibilities might make things go smoother at the meeting. For example: "I'm sure we can both find some areas for compromise." Or, "We may be able to put our heads together and find a new approach to carry to top management."

Best Tip

Prior to a meeting, send a memo or 'point paper' that outlines the issues at stake. It can clarify or even influence.

5. Prepare for the meeting. One good move is to try to get a reaction to your memo. A telephone call might be the best approach: "Thought I'd give you a quick call, see how you are thinking about the issue." For best results, the memo should have stated you'd be calling.

After getting some indication of where your opponent stands, it's time to prepare new arguments, decide how you might compromise or collaborate, and decide what you'll do if things bog down. Your goal should be: No one loses at this meeting—at least not me!

Do These Things at the Meeting

1. Set an upbeat tone. Reinforce the good tone established during the pre-meeting steps (memo, phone call). Helpful words: "Our contacts since the last meeting may have helped a bit to bring us together. But we still have areas of disagreement. Let's talk about them. I'm sure we can find a way to move forward."

2. Restate key positions. Even though you exchanged ideas at earlier meetings, and through memos and phone conversations, it is still important to summarize where things stand. Busy people have many things to do. This conflict situation may not be the most important thing on your opponent's mind. Clarity on current status is important to progress. The only way to be sure of such clarity is to summarize key points.

3. Follow your game plan on styles and arguments. You devoted a lot of pre-meeting time to thinking out the most appropriate styles and specific arguments to use. Ultimately, you'll want to be flexible and go with things that seem to be working. But not immediately. At the start of the meeting, stay with the plan. If it is well developed, it offers the best chance for success. Don't abandon it prematurely.

Never forget that you have a powerful ally forever at your disposal: persistence.

4. Quit temporarily if you reach an impasse. Use the avoidance style if a total impasse exists. The only other choice is to lose—and that's always unacceptable. If you find no way to move forward, the best option might be to suggest (as pleasantly as possible) that you suspend talks until you both can think through the blocking points in more detail.

This isn't a defeat for either party. And it shouldn't be regarded as such. Suspending talks gracefully may require you to educate your opponent, who may not have considered a temporary suspension (i.e., avoidance strategy). Helpful words: "I don't think we ought to try further to solve this today. Some new issues have been raised. I think we all need some time to consider them. I know I do."

5. Seek agreement on a next step. Once you both agree to suspend discussions temporarily, the obvious question is: What's next? Never leave such a meeting without an agreement on the next form of contact: memo, phone call, meeting. This signals that the problem is still open to being solved.

Regroup and Recycle

If the steps suggested in this chapter have been unsuccessful in resolving the conflict, and you feel that there is a glimmer of hope left, regroup and recycle through the steps again. You'll need new ideas, new arguments. But all your previous experience with this person and this issue should help you come up with them. Your knowledge of the process will help you also. You know the steps to take in a redesign. That structure will give you an edge. Further, persistence alone is often a powerful ally.

The Agile Manager's Checklist

✔ Repair any bad relationships before tackling conflict issues.

✔ Know the nature and cause of the conflict.

✔ Consider any possible further use of influence.

✔ Back off power positions that aren't working.

✔ Identify the right conflict management styles to use.

✔ Do the pre-meeting homework:

Establish a good tone/atmosphere.

Lay your cards on the table: Write a memo in advance, stating your case and educating.

Get a reaction to your memo before the meeting.

✔ At the meeting: Build on relationships established, restate your position, follow your game plan, and suggest suspension (temporarily) if impasse occurs.

✔ Seek agreement on the next step—and always have a next move!

SECTION VI

Put It All Together

"Let us never negotiate out of fear, but let us never fear to negotiate."

JOHN F. KENNEDY
INAUGURAL ADDRESS, JANUARY 20, 1961

"Never give in, never give in, never, never, never—in nothing great or small, large or petty—never give in except to convictions of honor and good sense."

WINSTON CHURCHILL
ADDRESS AT HARROW SCHOOL, OCTOBER 29, 1941

"Genius is one percent inspiration and 99 percent perspiration."

THOMAS EDISON
LIFE (1932) CHAPTER 24

Chapter Nine

Capture and Apply
The Tools

The Agile Manager sat in his home office on a nice Saturday afternoon. The rest of his family went away for the day so he could plan his Monday meeting with Ellen Taylor.

"I hate even thinking about this meeting," he thought to himself as he pushed aside a paper on which he'd answered the ten questions on influencing. "Elliot and Sims were tough, but Ellen will be even tougher. She's super smart and she's used to getting her way. She's already let me know she won't give an inch on marketing costs—and that's an area I think has the most to give. And she's casually mentioned her friend 'John at headquarters,' who just happens to be the senior vp for marketing.

"I'll get through it somehow," he continued to think. "One thing I've learned over the years is how important it is to strategize deliberately. Having tools and a comprehensive system as a guide sure helps."

He sighed and picked up a clean sheet of paper, wrote "Power Bases" along the top, and began writing words in a vertical column: Legitimate, Reward, Coercive, Connection . . .

The purpose of this chapter is to review and capture all the tools in one place—as a convenience for when you apply them. To start, refer to the diagram of the negotiation process on page 11.

I'll move you through the seven steps in an abbreviated fashion, apply them in a case example, and then encourage you to apply them to a personal negotiation situation.

Summary of Tools

1. Clarify Your Purpose. This is your long-range purpose. You may need to have multiple meetings with short-term goals. But in this first step, identify the ultimate objective of the negotiation.

2. Identify the Right Person to Approach. It may be necessary to deal with many people to accomplish your purpose. But name the first target person—and be sure that's the right place to start.

3. Assess the Negotiation Situation. Address the ten negotiation considerations:

- Nature of the Disagreement or Issue—The precise points of dispute.
- Level of Conflict—The degree of intensity of the fight.
- Priority of the Issue—Its relative importance and any risks in addressing it now.
- Characteristics of Your Opponent—Those qualities that will make the negotiation easy or hard.
- Relative Power Position—The likelihood of power differences being an advantage or disadvantage in the negotiation.
- Status and Importance of the Relationship—The history of the relationship, its importance for the future, and any risk the negotiation poses to it.
- Objectives—The optimum and acceptable range of outcomes for each party, and the areas of overlap where agreement might be possible.
- Opportunity for Creative Solutions—The search for a bigger pie, to achieve a win-win solution.
- Impact of Losing—Any downside to losing so critical that negotiation now must be avoided.
- Impact of Winning—Any unacceptable downside to winning.

What you'd like is a clear issue, a reasonable person to deal with, mutual flexibility in desired outcomes, some win-win opportunities, and no unacceptable downside to winning or losing. You may not satisfy all the considerations. But a deliberate examination of each should tell you if it's safe to proceed.

4. Try Using Influence. Influence is in this book's title because it is central to effective negotiation—and it is too often neglected. Successful influence efforts build commitment to the solution. Put it center stage. To do that, do three things:

Implement the process activities:

- *Lobbying*—Identify all bases to be touched.
- *Negotiating*—Skillful one-on-one bargaining.
- *Networking*—Use of a third party to help, if necessary.
- *Assessing Our Constituency*—Keep track of support and opposition.

Use the influence styles as categories to find arguments:

- *Logic*—Facts and cost/benefit arguments.
- *Common Vision*—Futuristic arguments that appeal to values and emotions.
- *Mutual Participation*—Joint development of an acceptable solution.

Use the Influence Tool to develop the influence plan:

—Whom do I want to influence?

—In what order should I approach people?

—What do I want to happen (at each encounter)?

—What's the target person like?

—What influence styles should I use?

—What actual arguments should I use?

—What conflict should I expect?

—How should I deal with the conflict?

—What meeting arrangements must I make? (Where, when, pre-work necessary etc.)

—How can I polish my act? (Test on peers—and practice.)

Influence is not a bad word. In our context, it is not in the least manipulative. Influence is simply a process of thinking through another's needs skillfully and designing arguments to meet those needs. The goal is to persuade the other person to believe in your proposed course of action. It won't always work—but it is a necessary step in an effective negotiation process. And it's always worth the effort.

   5. Apply Power if Influence Fails. Power sometimes has a negative connotation. But it is a necessary tool of leadership. To lead, you must be able to move others in the direction of your vision. When influence fails, power is the only option. And influence will never be successful with all people in all situations. Hence power is essential.

   When considering the use of power, do three things.

   A. Recall the meaning of power: It is your capacity to get your way because others respect your position or your personal qualities.

   B. Accurately assess your power resources. The types of power you may possess include:

Position Power
   .. Legitimate Power—due to your title.
   .. Reward Power—due to your ability to reward.
   .. Coercive Power—due to your capacity to punish or with-
      hold rewards.

Personal Power
   .. Expert Power—due to your special knowledge or skill.
   .. Connection Power—due to your special relationship to
      others.
   .. Referent Power—due to your charisma or personal at-
      tractiveness to others.

   C. Use the Power Tools (ten questions)

   —What are my objectives (both substance and relationship)?
   —Do I need to use power now (have I exhausted influence
      efforts)?
   —What power bases or sources do I have available?
   —Is it OK to use power in my organization?
   —What's the other person like (what type power might be
      most effective)?

—What is my personal relationship with the other person (does it make the use of power inappropriate)?

—What power bases should I use, and what specific arguments should I make?

—What conflict should I expect, and how should I deal with it?

—What administrative arrangements must be made?

—What do I do if things bog down?

Remember, you don't want to use power if it is not appropriate. So assess things carefully— your available power and its suitability in your organization and with this particular person. And just as with influence efforts, prepare thoroughly and be ready for potential conflict.

6. Manage Conflict Throughout the Process. Bad interpersonal relations and/or conflict may occur anywhere in the negotiation process. If relationships are a problem, tend to that before addressing conflict.

Conflict is simply a difference in viewpoint between two individuals over a given issue at a given point in time. It is inevitable and useful for creativity. But it must be managed.

In managing conflict, do three things:

A. Ensure that you are treating the right problem. Is it conflict, or could it be a case of bad interpersonal relations?

B. Select one of the conflict-management styles.

- Competition
- Avoidance
- Compromise
- Accommodation
- Collaboration

Which would be most effective in this situation?

C. Use the Conflict Management Tools (questions to consider, things to do prior to meeting, things to do at the meeting).

Questions to Consider

..What exactly do we disagree about?

..Why do we disagree (is it over means or ends)?

.. Have I exhausted efforts to educate (influence) the other person? If not, plan a new effort.

.. Have I antagonized the other person through an inappropriate use of power? If so, mend fences.

.. What's the other person like? How does he/she deal with conflict? What styles should I use?

Things to Do Prior to Meeting

.. Request a meeting (with the appropriate tone).

.. Be candid about the reason for meeting (to resolve a conflict).

.. Lay your cards on the table (maybe in a memo prior to the meeting).

.. Educate the other person on the conflict-management styles (he or she may not know them).

.. Prepare for the meeting (maybe by a phone call to get a reaction to your memo).

Things to Do at the Meeting

.. Set an upbeat tone.

.. Restate key positions.

.. Follow the game plan on styles/arguments.

.. Quit temporarily if an impasse occurs (suggest coming back later to resolve the conflict).

.. Seek agreement on a next step (always plan a next move).

7. Achieve an Acceptable Solution or Reassess Your Effort. The last step in the process is to ensure that the outcome is acceptable. If it isn't, think back through the whole process and redesign your approach.

Apply the Tools: A Case Study

Situation: To test your ability to apply the tools, read the situation and dialogue that follows. Then, before reading my comments, ask yourself the following questions:

1. Was the climate for negotiating favorable or unfavorable?
2. Was this a good influence effort? Why?
3. What were the major strengths and weaknesses of the effort?

A fire chief of a large metropolitan fire department, Mark,

would like to influence the Union President, Patrick, to support (with the union members) a proposed set of physical agility standards for all firefighters.

Patrick is relatively new. He has a reputation for being reasonable to do business with. Mark has had a few social contacts with him, but he doesn't know him well enough yet to judge how he'll react on a major professional issue like this one—modifying a contract with a big impact on union members.

Mark decides that calling an exploratory meeting to get an early reaction on this issue might be best. He sends Patrick a short letter requesting a meeting to discuss the possibility of support for the new standards. He attaches a copy of the standards.

The scene is Patrick's office, the day of their meeting.

Patrick: Good morning, Mark. Nice to see you.

Mark: All settled in by now?

Patrick: Slowly, but surely. I got your letter.

Mark: What do you think?

Patrick: Well, I think it's going to take a lot of doing to get members to support this.

Mark: Why do you think that? These standards are similar to what you'd find in many large departments.

Patrick: Perhaps—but I circulated this to some key members, opinion formers. They don't think these standards are a good match with the requirements of the job—just not valid and predictive from a job-related perspective.

Mark: I agree with them in part. But you can't ever look at specific standards in isolation and find a perfect match with the job requirements.

Patrick: Then why have them?

Mark: The standards have to be viewed as a total list of abilities—and as the outcome of a physical training program that is designed to help people meet the standards and that has a lot of additional, related benefits.

Patrick: Like what?

Mark: Like better general health, reduced group insurance costs, fewer accidents, reduced absenteeism due to sickness—even improved morale. And, of course, enhanced job performance, particularly in physically demanding situations.

Patrick: Can we document the advantages?

Mark: Absolutely. I've talked to fire chiefs all over the country in putting these standards together. Everyone is so enthusiastic about them. I've got all the evidence assembled. It's very convincing. I can put it together for you.

Patrick: I'd like to see it.

Mark: And you will. I didn't want to flood you with information for this meeting—really just wanted to know if you'd be receptive to exploring the idea.

Patrick: Well, I am—but I need facts.

Mark: Let me suggest that you and I each appoint three people to wrestle with this. I'll turn all the supporting facts over to them. Let them examine the facts, check them with anyone they wish, and then you and I can meet with them to get their suggestions. Then we'll decide what to do next.

Patrick: I like it. You be the focal point. I'll get you three really sharp people to work with. Set up the committee. Keep me posted.

Mark: Thanks. I'll stay in touch as we proceed.

Comments:

1. Assessing the negotiation climate indicates a reasonable chance of success.

- It's a clear issue
- There's a low level of conflict
- It's an important matter
- Both opponents are reasonable
- There are no power problems
- There's an opportunity to negotiate a compromise solution

- There is no big downside to winning or losing

2. Influence is the proper place to start.

3. When you don't know the influencee well, exploratory sessions, though time consuming, can be useful—everybody gets educated. Mark made the right move here.

4. Mark gave every indication of having done his homework.

5. It was not necessary or appropriate to lay out all the facts at this time.

6. The joint committee idea is an example of mutual participation. Hopefully, it will succeed. Even if it fails, Mark and Patrick can always meet personally to try to agree on a solution.

7. This influence effort may take time, because the participants are strangers to one another. But if Mark remains patient, he will maximize his chance of success.

8. If influence fails, Mark can consider the use of power. He'll find he does have power resources—though he may choose to not use them on this issue. After all, he'll be doing a lot of business with Patrick in the future.

Try the Tools Yourself

The case example you just read should be helpful as a first approach to an application. However, the best way to capture the tools, to really make them your own, is to apply them to a personal case in your own world.

I would encourage you to do just that—and to do it now, while the material is fresh in your mind.

You have all the tools assembled conveniently in this chapter. Try focusing those tools on some pressing matter in your life—something you care a lot about.

- Assess the opportunity to negotiate.
- Develop a detailed influence plan.
- Think out your power options in advance.
- Consider how you might deal with likely conflicts.

Then do it! Put your plan into action. I hope the tools give you the edge to win. I'll bet you do. Good luck!